HOW TO START A FOOD TRUCK BUSINESS FOR BEGINNERS TO PRO

A Practical Guide to Launching and Managing a Thriving Food Truck Business with Complete Step-by-Step Instructions and Expert Tips to Avoid Common Pitfalls

Durrant Weber Robert

Copyright © 2024

All Rights Are Reserved

The content in this book may not be reproduced, duplicated, or transferred without the express written permission of the author or publisher. Under no circumstances will the publisher or author be held liable or legally responsible for any losses, expenditures, or damages incurred directly or indirectly as a consequence of the information included in this book.

Legal Remarks

Copyright protection applies to this publication. It is only intended for personal use. No piece of this work may be modified, distributed, sold, quoted, or paraphrased without the author's or publisher's consent.

Disclaimer Statement

Please keep in mind that the contents of this booklet are meant for educational and recreational purposes. Every effort has been made to offer accurate, up-to-date, reliable, and thorough information. There are, however, no stated or implied assurances of any kind. Readers understand that the author is providing competent counsel. The content in this book originates from several sources. Please seek the opinion of a competent professional before using any of the tactics outlined in this book. By reading this book, the reader agrees that the author will not be held accountable for any direct or indirect damages resulting from the use of the information contained therein, including, but not limited to, errors, omissions, or inaccuracies.

TABLE OF CONTENTS

INTRODUCTION 5
   Why Start a Food Truck Business? 5
   Benefits and Challenges of Running a Food Truck 6

UNDERSTANDING THE FOOD TRUCK INDUSTRY 9
   Overview of the Food Truck Market 9
   Trends and Opportunities 11
   Legal and Regulatory Considerations 13

PLANNING YOUR FOOD TRUCK BUSINESS 16
   Defining Your Concept and Menu 16
   Developing a Business Plan 17
   Financing Your Food Truck 19

SETTING UP YOUR FOOD TRUCK 22
   Choosing the Right Truck or Trailer 22
   Equipment and Supplies 23
   Designing Your Food Truck 25

NAVIGATING PERMITS, LICENSES, AND REGULATIONS .. 28
   Obtaining Permits and Licenses 28
   Health and Safety Regulations 29
   Insurance for Your Food Truck Business 31

SOURCING INGREDIENTS AND SUPPLIERS 33
   Finding Quality Ingredients 33
   Building Relationships with Suppliers 34
   Managing Inventory 36

MARKETING AND BRANDING YOUR FOOD TRUCK 39
   Creating a Unique Brand Identity 39

- Social Media and Online Presence 40
- Promotions and Marketing Strategies 41
- **MANAGING OPERATIONS** **44**
  - Staffing Your Food Truck 45
  - Customer Service and Engagement 47
  - Managing Finances and Budgeting 49
- **GROWING YOUR FOOD TRUCK BUSINESS** **51**
  - Adding Additional Locations or Trucks 52
  - Building a loyal customer base 54
- **ADAPTING TO CHALLENGES AND TRENDS** **56**
  - Dealing with Seasonality and Weather 57
  - Staying Ahead of Food Trends 58
  - Overcoming Common Challenges in the Food Truck Industry 60
- **CONCLUSION** **63**

INTRODUCTION

Why Start a Food Truck Business?

Starting a food truck business is like embarking on a culinary adventure. Picture this: the sizzle of your signature dish, the aroma wafting through the air, and the excited chatter of customers lining up for a taste of your creations. It's a journey filled with flavors, challenges, and ultimately, the satisfaction of turning your passion for food into a thriving business. In this book, "How to Start a Food Truck Business from Beginner to Pro," we'll take you through every step of this exciting journey. Whether you're a food enthusiast dreaming of sharing your recipes with the world or a seasoned chef looking to take your talents on the road, this book is your roadmap to success in the competitive world of food trucks.

Before we dive into the nitty-gritty details, let's set the stage by exploring why starting a food truck business is such a tantalizing prospect. Imagine being your boss, setting your hours, and having the freedom to experiment with different cuisines and flavors—all while bringing joy to your customers' taste buds.

But let's not sugarcoat it: running a food truck is no cakewalk (pun intended). It requires meticulous planning, hard work, and a dash of creativity. From securing permits and licenses to designing your truck and crafting a mouthwatering menu, there's a lot to consider before you can hit the streets and start serving up delicious dishes.

One of the most exciting aspects of starting a food truck business is the endless possibilities for creativity and innovation. You have the freedom to experiment with different cuisines, flavors, and concepts, and to constantly evolve your menu based on customer feedback and market trends.

Of course, no culinary adventure would be complete without its fair share of challenges. From navigating complex regulations to dealing with unpredictable weather and competition, running a food truck requires resilience, adaptability, and a willingness to learn from both successes and setbacks.

But fear not, aspiring food truck entrepreneurs! This book is your ultimate guide to overcoming these challenges and building a successful food truck business from the ground up. Whether you're just starting or looking to take your existing food truck to the next level, we've got you covered with practical tips, expert advice, and real-life success stories to inspire and motivate you along the way.

So, grab your apron, fire up the grill, and get ready to embark on the culinary adventure of a lifetime. Your food truck journey starts here, and we can't wait to see where it takes you!

Benefits and Challenges of Running a Food Truck

Imagine waking up to the tantalizing smell of sizzling bacon and freshly brewed coffee, the sound of early risers chatting excitedly as they wait for their morning pick-me-up. Now, picture yourself at the heart of this bustling scene, the proud owner of a food truck, serving up delicious meals on wheels to eager customers. Welcome to the world of food trucks, where every day is an adventure in flavor and every meal is a chance to make someone's day a little brighter.

In this book, we're going to take you on a journey through the vibrant and dynamic world of food trucks. We'll explore the benefits of running a food truck, from the freedom to be your boss to the opportunity to bring your culinary creations to a wide and diverse audience. But we'll also delve into the challenges you'll face along the way, from navigating complex regulations to dealing with fickle weather and fierce competition.

Let's start with the benefits. One of the biggest advantages of running a food truck is the freedom it offers. Unlike a traditional brick-and-mortar restaurant, a food truck allows you to take your kitchen on the road, bringing your food to where the hungry crowds are. This flexibility means you can cater at festivals, and events, or even just park in popular spots around town, ensuring a steady stream of customers and keeping things exciting and dynamic.

Another major benefit of running a food truck is the lower startup costs compared to a traditional restaurant. With a food truck, you can skip the hefty overheads associated with renting or buying a commercial space and instead invest in a vehicle and kitchen equipment. This lower barrier to entry makes it easier for aspiring chefs and food entrepreneurs to turn their dreams into reality.

But of course, running a food truck isn't all sunshine and rainbows. There are plenty of challenges you'll need to overcome along the way. One of the biggest hurdles is navigating the complex web of regulations and permits that govern the food truck industry. From health and safety regulations to zoning laws and parking restrictions, there's a lot to consider before you can hit the road and start serving up your culinary delights.

Then there's the issue of competition. The food truck scene is more popular than ever, which means you'll be facing stiff competition from other trucks vying for the same customers. To stand out from the crowd, you'll need to get creative with your menu, marketing, and branding, and constantly innovate to keep your customers coming back for more.

But despite these challenges, the rewards of running a food truck are well worth it. The thrill of seeing your customers' faces light up as they take their first bite of your signature dish, the satisfaction of knowing you're bringing joy to people's lives through your food, and the sense of pride that comes from building a successful business from the ground up – these are just a few of the reasons why running a food truck is such a rewarding and fulfilling endeavor.

So, if you're ready to embark on a culinary adventure like no other, join us as we explore the world of food trucks and discover what it takes to turn your passion for food into a thriving business. The road ahead may be challenging, but with the right attitude, determination, and a sprinkle of creativity, the sky's the limit for your food truck dreams. Let's hit the road and start cooking up a storm!

UNDERSTANDING THE FOOD TRUCK INDUSTRY

Overview of the Food Truck Market

The food truck market is a dynamic and thriving industry that has experienced tremendous growth in recent years. From bustling city streets to local festivals and events, food trucks have become a popular choice for people looking for convenient and delicious meals on the go. In this chapter, we'll take a closer look at the food truck market, exploring its growth drivers, key trends, and future outlook.

Market Size and Growth

The food truck market has grown significantly over the past decade, fueled by changing consumer preferences and a growing demand for convenient, high-quality food options. According to industry reports, the global food truck market was valued at over $1 billion in 2020 and is projected to continue growing at a compound annual growth rate (CAGR) of around 5% from 2021 to 2026.

Key Drivers of Growth

Several factors have contributed to the growth of the food truck market. One of the key drivers is the rise of the "foodie" culture, with more people seeking out unique and innovative food experiences. Food trucks offer a wide variety of cuisines and flavors, making them a popular choice for adventurous eaters looking to try something new.

Changing Consumer Preferences

Consumer preferences have also played a significant role in the growth of the food truck market. Today's consumers are looking for more than just a meal – they want an experience. Food trucks often provide a more interactive and engaging dining experience compared to traditional restaurants, with customers able to watch their food being prepared fresh on the spot.

Impact of COVID-19

The COVID-19 pandemic had a significant impact on the food truck market, with many operators forced to close temporarily due to lockdowns and restrictions on public gatherings. However, as restrictions have eased, many food truck operators have adapted their businesses to meet the changing needs of consumers, such as offering online ordering and contactless payment options.

Key Trends in the Food Truck Market

Several key trends are shaping the food truck market. One of the most notable trends is the focus on health and wellness. Many food truck operators are now offering healthier menu options, such as plant-based dishes and low-sugar alternatives, to cater to the growing demand for healthier food choices.

Technology and Innovation

Technology is also playing an increasingly important role in the food truck market. Many operators are using technology to streamline operations, such as using mobile apps for ordering and payment processing. Some food trucks are even using advanced cooking equipment, such as sous vide machines and smoker ovens, to create gourmet dishes on the go.

Future Outlook

Looking ahead, the future looks bright for the food truck market. As consumer preferences continue to evolve, food truck operators will need to stay ahead of the curve by offering innovative menu options, embracing technology, and providing exceptional customer experiences. With the right strategy and approach, food trucks have the potential to continue thriving and delight customers for years to come.

Trends and Opportunities

The world of food trucks is constantly evolving, with new trends and opportunities emerging all the time. Whether you're just starting or looking to take your food truck business to the next level, it's important to stay informed about the latest developments in the industry. In this chapter, we'll explore some of the current trends and opportunities in the food truck market, and how you can leverage them to succeed in your own food truck business.

One of the most exciting trends in the food truck industry is the rise of gourmet and artisanal food trucks. Gone are the days when food trucks were limited to serving simple, street food-style fare. Today, food trucks are offering gourmet dishes that rival those found in high-end restaurants, using high-quality ingredients and innovative cooking techniques to create dishes that are as delicious as they are Instagram-worthy.

Another trend that's gaining traction in the food truck industry is the focus on health and wellness. With more people becoming conscious of their dietary choices, food truck operators are responding by offering healthier menu options, such as plant-based dishes, gluten-free alternatives, and low-sugar treats. By catering to this growing demand for healthier food choices, food truck operators can attract a wider customer base and differentiate themselves from the competition.

Technology is also playing a significant role in shaping the future of the food truck industry. Many food truck operators are using technology to streamline their operations and enhance the customer experience. For example, some food trucks are using mobile apps for ordering and payment processing, allowing customers to place orders and pay for their meals without having to wait in line. Other food trucks are using social media platforms to engage with their customers and promote their businesses, using platforms like Instagram and Facebook to share mouth-watering photos of their dishes and announce their locations.

In addition to these trends, there are also several exciting opportunities emerging in the food truck industry. One of the biggest opportunities is the growing demand for food trucks at events and festivals. As more people seek out unique and memorable dining experiences, food trucks are becoming a popular choice for catering at weddings, corporate events, and music festivals. By tapping into this demand, food truck operators can increase their revenue and exposure, while also building relationships with event organizers and other vendors.

Another opportunity in the food truck industry is the ability to experiment and innovate with your menu. Unlike traditional restaurants, food trucks offer a relatively low-cost way to test out new dishes and concepts, allowing you to quickly adapt to changing tastes and preferences. By staying ahead of the curve and offering innovative menu options, you can attract new customers and keep them coming back for more.

Legal and Regulatory Considerations

In the world of food truck entrepreneurship, understanding and navigating the legal and regulatory landscape is crucial. From obtaining permits and licenses to complying with health and safety regulations, there are several key considerations that every food truck operator must be aware of. In this chapter, we'll explore the legal and regulatory considerations that are essential for starting and running a successful food truck business.

Permits and Licenses

One of the first steps in starting a food truck business is obtaining the necessary permits and licenses. These can vary depending on your location, so it's important to research the requirements in your area. Typically, you'll need a business license, a food service permit, and a parking permit for your food truck. In some cases, you may also need additional permits for things like outdoor seating or selling alcohol.

Health and Safety Regulations

Ensuring the health and safety of your customers is paramount when running a food truck. This means complying with food safety regulations, such as proper food handling and storage practices, as well as regular health inspections. It's also important to have the appropriate insurance coverage to protect your business in the event of any accidents or liabilities.

Zoning and Parking Regulations

Another important consideration for food truck operators is zoning and parking regulations. These can dictate where you're allowed to operate your food truck and for how long. It's important to research the zoning laws in your area to ensure that you're operating legally and to avoid any potential fines or penalties.

Tax Considerations

Like any other business, food truck operators are subject to various tax obligations. This includes income tax, sales tax, and potentially other taxes depending on your location. It's important to keep accurate records of your income and expenses and to consult with a tax professional to ensure that you're meeting all of your tax obligations.

Contractual Agreements

When starting a food truck business, you may also need to enter into contractual agreements with suppliers, vendors, and other partners. It's important to carefully review and negotiate these agreements to protect your interests and ensure that you're not entering into any unfavorable terms.

Compliance with Local Laws and Regulations

Finally, it's important to stay informed about any changes or updates to local laws and regulations that may affect your food truck business. This includes things like changes to health and safety regulations, zoning laws, or tax laws. By staying informed and proactive, you can ensure that your food truck business remains compliant and successful.

Understanding and navigating the legal and regulatory landscape is essential for starting and running a successful food truck business. By taking the time to research and comply with the necessary permits, licenses, and regulations, you can set your food truck business up for success and avoid any potential legal issues down the road.

PLANNING YOUR FOOD TRUCK BUSINESS

Defining Your Concept and Menu

Imagine stepping up to your food truck, the aroma of your signature dish wafting through the air, and the eager faces of customers awaiting their first bite. Your food truck concept is more than just a menu – it's an experience. It's about defining what makes your food truck unique and creating a concept that resonates with your target audience.

Understanding Your Vision

Your concept should reflect your vision for your food truck business. Are you passionate about bringing a taste of your cultural heritage to the streets? Or perhaps you're focused on offering healthier alternatives to traditional fast food. Whatever your vision, it should be the driving force behind your concept and menu.

Researching Your Market and Audience

Before finalizing your concept, it's crucial to research your market and audience. What are the popular food trends in your area? Who is your target audience, and what are their preferences? By understanding your market and audience, you can tailor your concept and menu to meet their needs and preferences.

Creating a Memorable Menu

Your menu is the heart of your food truck concept. It should showcase your unique offerings while appealing to a broad audience. Consider offering a mix of familiar favorites and innovative dishes to cater to different tastes. It's also important to keep your menu flexible, allowing for seasonal changes and special promotions.

Testing and Refining Your Concept

Once you've developed your concept and menu, it's time to put them to the test. Consider hosting a soft launch or pop-up event to gather feedback from customers. Use this feedback to refine your concept and menu, ensuring that they resonate with your target audience.

Building Your Brand Identity

Your concept should not only be reflected in your menu but also your brand identity. Consider how you can use branding elements such as your logo, colors, and messaging to convey your concept and values to your customers.

Developing a Business Plan

Developing a solid business plan is essential for any aspiring food truck entrepreneur. It's your roadmap to success, guiding you through the process of starting and running your food truck business. In this chapter, we'll explore the key elements of a business plan and how to create one that sets you up for success.

Setting Your Goals and Objectives

The first step in developing a business plan is to define your goals and objectives. What do you hope to achieve with your food truck business? Are you looking to build a successful business that supports you financially, or are you more focused on creating a unique culinary experience for your customers? By setting clear and achievable goals, you can create a roadmap for your business that keeps you focused and motivated.

Market Analysis

A thorough market analysis is crucial for understanding your industry, competitors, and target market. Research the food truck industry in your area, including trends, customer preferences, and potential competitors. Identify your target market and how you plan to reach them. Understanding the market will help you position your food truck business for success.

Menu Planning and Pricing

Your menu is the centerpiece of your food truck business, so it's important to plan it carefully. Consider your target market, industry trends, and your culinary expertise when designing your menu. Pricing is also key – you'll need to set prices that are competitive yet profitable. By carefully planning your menu and pricing, you can attract customers and maximize profits.

Marketing and Promotion

Marketing and promotion are essential for attracting customers to your food truck. Consider how you will promote your business, such as through social media, local events, or partnerships with other businesses. Develop a marketing strategy that helps you reach your target market and build a loyal customer base.

Financial Planning

A solid financial plan is crucial for the success of your food truck business. Estimate your startup costs, including the cost of purchasing or renting a truck, equipment, and licenses. Develop a budget that outlines your expected expenses and projected income. This will help you understand the financial feasibility of your business and plan accordingly.

Operations Plan

Your operations plan outlines how you will run your food truck business on a day-to-day basis. This includes details such as your location, hours of operation, staffing requirements, and inventory management. By carefully planning your operations, you can ensure that your business runs smoothly and efficiently.

Risk Management

Every business faces risks, and it's important to identify and mitigate them as much as possible. Consider potential risks to your food truck business, such as food safety issues, equipment breakdowns, or inclement weather. Develop a plan for how you will manage these risks to minimize their impact on your business.

Financing Your Food Truck

Financing your food truck is a crucial step in turning your culinary dreams into reality. In this chapter, we'll explore the various options for financing your food truck, from traditional loans to crowdfunding, and how to choose the right option for your business.

Assessing Your Financial Needs

Before you can begin financing your food truck, you need to determine how much money you'll need to get started. This includes the cost of purchasing or leasing a food truck, equipment, permits, licenses, and initial operating expenses. By assessing your financial needs upfront, you can create a realistic budget and avoid surprises down the road.

Traditional Loans

One of the most common ways to finance a food truck is through a traditional loan from a bank or financial institution. These loans typically require a strong credit history and a solid business plan. They can be used to cover the cost of purchasing a food truck, equipment, and other startup expenses. However, getting approved for a traditional loan can be challenging, especially for new entrepreneurs.

SBA Loans

Another option for financing your food truck is an SBA loan, which is backed by the Small Business Administration. These loans offer competitive interest rates and flexible repayment terms, making them an attractive option for many food truck entrepreneurs. However, SBA loans also require a strong credit history and a detailed business plan.

Crowdfunding

Crowdfunding has become a popular way to raise money for all types of businesses, including food trucks. Platforms like Kickstarter and Indiegogo allow you to create a campaign to raise funds from a large number of people. This can be a great way to generate buzz for your food truck business and raise the capital you need to get started. However, crowdfunding campaigns require a lot of planning and effort to be successful.

Grants and Contests

There are also several grants and contests specifically for food truck entrepreneurs. These can be a great way to secure funding without taking on debt. However, competition for grants and contests can be fierce, so it's important to research and apply early.

Family and Friends

Finally, don't overlook the possibility of borrowing money from family and friends. This can be a less formal option than traditional loans, but it's still important to treat it as a business transaction and to have clear terms and expectations in place.

SETTING UP YOUR FOOD TRUCK

Choosing the Right Truck or Trailer

Choosing the right truck or trailer for your food truck business is a crucial decision that can impact your success. In this chapter, we'll explore the factors to consider when selecting a vehicle, from size and layout to cost and maintenance, to help you make an informed choice that aligns with your business goals.

Size and Layout

The size and layout of your food truck will depend on the type of cuisine you plan to serve and the equipment you need. Consider the space you'll need for cooking, prep work, storage, and serving. A larger truck may offer more space for equipment and storage, but it may also be more expensive to operate and maintain.

Cost and Budget

Budget is a key consideration when choosing a food truck. Determine how much you can afford to spend on a vehicle, including the cost of purchasing or leasing, outfitting, and customizing. Keep in mind that you'll also need to budget for permits, licenses, insurance, and other startup costs.

Condition and Maintenance

The condition of the truck is another important factor to consider. A new truck may be more reliable and require less maintenance, but it will also be more expensive. A used truck may be more affordable, but it may require more maintenance and repairs. Consider the age, mileage, and maintenance history of the truck when making your decision.

Customization and Branding

Customizing your food truck to reflect your brand and attract customers is an important consideration. Consider how you can customize the exterior and interior of the truck to make it stand out and create a memorable experience for your customers. This may include adding signage, graphics, and branding elements that reflect your brand identity.

Fuel Efficiency and Environmental Impact

Fuel efficiency is another important factor to consider, especially if you plan to operate your food truck frequently. Look for a vehicle that is fuel-efficient and has a low environmental impact. This can help you save money on fuel costs and reduce your carbon footprint.

Accessibility and Safety

Finally, consider the accessibility and safety of the truck. Ensure that the truck is easy to access for both you and your customers and that it meets all safety regulations and requirements. This includes having the necessary safety equipment, such as fire extinguishers and first aid kits, and ensuring that the vehicle is in good working condition.

Equipment and Supplies

Equipping your food truck with the right tools and supplies is like assembling a culinary toolbox – each item serving a specific purpose to help you craft delicious meals and run your business smoothly. In this chapter, we'll explore the essential equipment and supplies you need to outfit your food truck kitchen, from cooking appliances to serving tools, ensuring you're well-prepared to serve up culinary delights on the go.

The Heart of Your Kitchen: Cooking Appliances

At the core of your food truck kitchen are the cooking appliances that bring your recipes to life. Consider appliances like grills, fryers, and ovens that match your menu needs and space constraints. Opt for energy-efficient models to save on operating costs and ensure they're easy to clean and maintain for efficient operation.

Tools of the Trade: Food Preparation Equipment

Efficient food preparation is key to keeping up with customer demand. Stock your kitchen with essential tools like cutting boards, knives, mixing bowls, and food storage containers. These items not only streamline your workflow but also contribute to food safety and quality.

Serving Up Success: Serving Tools and Utensils

Delivering your culinary creations to customers requires the right serving tools and utensils. Invest in durable, easy-to-clean items such as serving spoons, tongs, and spatulas, as well as plates, bowls, and utensils for customers. These items not only enhance the dining experience but also contribute to the overall efficiency of your operation.

To-Go Essentials: Packaging and Supplies

For customers on the move, you'll need packaging and to-go supplies that keep your food fresh and secure. Consider eco-friendly options for containers, bags, and utensils to align with sustainable practices and customer preferences. These items not only showcase your commitment to the environment but also enhance your brand image.

Keeping It Clean: Cleaning Supplies

Maintaining a clean and sanitary kitchen is paramount to your food truck's success. Stock up on cleaning supplies such as sanitizing wipes, disinfectant spray, and garbage bags to ensure your kitchen meets health and safety standards. Regular cleaning and maintenance help prevent foodborne illnesses and maintain a positive reputation.

Safety First: Safety Equipment

Safety should always be a top priority in your food truck kitchen. Equip your truck with essential safety equipment like fire extinguishers, first aid kits, and emergency exits to protect yourself and your customers. Regular inspections and maintenance ensure these items are always ready for use.

Designing Your Food Truck

Designing your food truck is more than just creating a vehicle for cooking and serving food – it's about creating a mobile culinary experience that delights your customers and sets you apart from the competition. In this chapter, we'll explore the key considerations when designing your food truck, from layout and branding to functionality and customer experience, to help you create a food truck that's as unique as your culinary vision.

Concept and Theme

Before diving into the details of your food truck design, it's important to establish a clear concept and theme. Your concept should reflect your brand identity and culinary vision, whether it's a retro diner on wheels or a sleek and modern gourmet kitchen. Consider how you can incorporate elements of your concept into every aspect of your food truck design, from the exterior to the interior decor.

Exterior Design

The exterior of your food truck is the first thing that customers will see, so it's important to make a good impression. Consider how you can use colors, graphics, and signage to grab attention and communicate your brand identity. You'll also need to consider practical aspects of the exterior design, such as the layout of windows and serving areas, as well as any additional features like awnings or signage.

Interior Layout

The layout of your food truck kitchen is critical for ensuring efficiency and productivity. Consider how you can optimize the space to streamline your workflow and minimize wasted movement. This includes the placement of cooking appliances, storage areas, and serving counters. A well-designed layout can help you prepare and serve food quickly and efficiently, even in a small space.

Branding and Identity

Branding is an important aspect of your food truck design, as it helps to create a cohesive and memorable experience for your customers. Consider how you can incorporate your logo, colors, and branding elements into every aspect of your food truck design, from the exterior to the packaging. Consistent branding helps to reinforce your brand identity and make your food truck stand out in a crowded market.

Functionality and Safety

In addition to aesthetics, it's important to consider the functionality and safety of your food truck design. Make sure that your kitchen layout allows for efficient food preparation and cooking, and that your serving areas are well-organized and easy to access. It's also important to ensure that your food truck meets all safety regulations and requirements, including fire safety and health codes.

Customer Experience

Finally, consider how your food truck design can enhance the overall customer experience. This includes aspects such as seating options, music, and lighting, as well as the overall ambiance of your food truck. Creating a welcoming and comfortable environment can help to attract customers and encourage them to return.

NAVIGATING PERMITS, LICENSES, AND REGULATIONS

Obtaining Permits and Licenses

Before you hit the road with your food truck, it's crucial to understand the permit and licensing requirements in your area. These requirements can vary widely depending on your location, so it's essential to research and familiarize yourself with the specific regulations that apply to your business. This includes obtaining the necessary permits and licenses from local health departments, fire departments, and other regulatory agencies.

Health Department Permits

One of the most important permits you'll need for your food truck is a health department permit. This permit is issued by the local health department and ensures that your food truck meets all health and safety standards. To obtain this permit, you'll likely need to undergo an inspection of your food truck and kitchen facilities to ensure they meet the required standards for cleanliness and food safety.

Fire Department Permits

In addition to a health department permit, you may also need a fire department permit for your food truck. This permit is issued by the local fire department and ensures that your food truck meets all fire safety standards. This may include requirements for fire extinguishers, emergency exits, and other safety equipment.

Business Licenses

In addition to permits, you'll also need to obtain a business license for your food truck. This license is issued by the local government and allows you to operate your food truck legally. The requirements for obtaining a business license can vary depending on your location, so it's important to research the specific requirements in your area.

Other Permits and Licenses

Depending on your location and the nature of your food truck business, you may also need other permits and licenses. This may include a food handler's permit for yourself and your employees, as well as a mobile food vendor permit. It's important to research and obtain all necessary permits and licenses to avoid legal issues that can jeopardize your business.

Obtaining permits and licenses for your food truck is a critical step in starting a successful business. By understanding the specific requirements in your area and ensuring that you comply with all regulations, you can operate your food truck legally and avoid potential pitfalls that can hinder your success. With the right permits and licenses in hand, you can hit the road with confidence, knowing that you're operating your food truck legally and responsibly.

Health and Safety Regulations

Proper food handling practices are essential for preventing foodborne illnesses and ensuring the safety of your customers. This includes practices such as washing hands regularly, using gloves when handling food, and storing food at the correct temperatures. By following these practices, you can minimize the risk of contamination and ensure that your food is safe to eat.

Sanitation Requirements

Maintaining a clean and sanitary food truck is critical for preventing the spread of germs and bacteria. This includes regularly cleaning and sanitizing all surfaces, equipment, and utensils, as well as ensuring that your water supply is clean and safe. By adhering to strict sanitation requirements, you can create a safe and hygienic environment for preparing and serving food.

Health Department Inspections

Food trucks are subject to regular inspections by the local health department to ensure compliance with health and safety regulations. Inspections typically focus on food storage, handling, and preparation practices, as well as the cleanliness of the food truck and its equipment. It's important to be prepared for these inspections and to address any issues that are identified promptly.

Allergen Management

Food allergies are a serious concern for many people, and it's important to take steps to prevent cross-contamination and ensure that customers with food allergies can safely enjoy your food. This includes clearly labeling allergens on your menu, using separate utensils and equipment for preparing allergen-free food, and training your staff on allergen management practices.

Training and Certification

Proper training and certification are essential for ensuring that you and your staff are knowledgeable about food safety practices. This includes obtaining a food handler's permit and ensuring that all staff members are trained in safe food handling practices. By investing in training and certification, you can demonstrate your commitment to food safety and protect the health of your customers.

Insurance for Your Food Truck Business

Operating a food truck comes with its own set of risks, from accidents on the road to food-related illnesses. In this chapter, we'll explore the importance of insurance for your food truck business, the types of insurance you may need, and how to find the right coverage to protect your business and your customers.

Understanding the Risks

Before diving into the details of insurance, it's important to understand the risks associated with operating a food truck. These risks can include accidents involving your truck, foodborne illnesses, and liability issues. By understanding these risks, you can better appreciate the importance of having the right insurance coverage in place.

Types of Insurance

Several types of insurance are important for food truck businesses:

1. **General Liability Insurance**: This type of insurance protects you against claims of bodily injury or property damage that occur as a result of your business operations. For example, if a customer slips and falls while visiting your food truck, general liability insurance would cover the costs of their medical expenses and any legal fees associated with the claim.

2. **Commercial Auto Insurance**: If you're using your truck for business purposes, you'll need commercial auto insurance to protect against accidents on the road. This type of insurance is similar to personal auto insurance but provides additional coverage for business use.
3. **Product Liability Insurance**: This insurance protects you in case someone becomes ill or is injured as a result of consuming your food. Product liability insurance can help cover legal fees and settlements if a customer sues you over a food-related illness or injury.
4. **Property Insurance**: Property insurance protects your food truck and its contents in case of damage or theft. This can include coverage for your truck, equipment, and inventory.
5. **Workers' Compensation Insurance**: If you have employees, workers' compensation insurance is required in most states. This insurance provides coverage for medical expenses and lost wages if an employee is injured on the job.

Finding the Right Coverage

Finding the right insurance coverage for your food truck business can be challenging, but it's essential to protect yourself and your investment. Start by researching insurance providers that specialize in food truck insurance. They will have a better understanding of the unique risks associated with your business and can help you find the right coverage at the right price.

SOURCING INGREDIENTS AND SUPPLIERS

Finding Quality Ingredients

Finding quality ingredients is essential for creating delicious and memorable dishes that keep your customers coming back for more. In this chapter, we'll explore the importance of sourcing high-quality ingredients for your food truck business, how to find the best suppliers and tips for ensuring the freshness and quality of your ingredients.

Importance of Quality Ingredients

Quality ingredients are the foundation of great food. They can elevate your dishes, enhance their flavors, and set your food truck apart from the competition. By using fresh, high-quality ingredients, you can create dishes that are not only delicious but also healthier and more satisfying for your customers.

Sourcing Suppliers

Finding the right suppliers for your ingredients is crucial for ensuring their quality and freshness. Look for suppliers that specialize in providing ingredients to food service businesses, as they will have a better understanding of your needs and can offer a wider variety of products. Local farmer's markets, specialty food stores, and online suppliers can also be great sources of high-quality ingredients.

Ensuring Freshness and Quality

Once you've found a supplier, it's important to ensure the freshness and quality of your ingredients. This includes inspecting the ingredients when they arrive, storing them properly, and using them before they expire. It's also important to develop relationships with your suppliers so that you can communicate your needs and preferences and ensure that you're getting the best products available.

Seasonal and Local Ingredients

Using seasonal and local ingredients is not only a great way to ensure freshness and quality but also to support local farmers and promote sustainability. Seasonal ingredients are often more flavorful and nutritious, as they are harvested at the peak of ripeness. Local ingredients also reduce the carbon footprint of your business and can be a great selling point for environmentally conscious customers.

Specialty and Ethnic Ingredients

Adding specialty and ethnic ingredients to your menu can help you create unique and flavorful dishes that set your food truck apart. Look for specialty food stores and online suppliers that offer a wide variety of ethnic ingredients, spices, and condiments. Experimenting with new ingredients can help you keep your menu fresh and exciting for your customers.

Building Relationships with Suppliers

Building strong relationships with your suppliers is crucial for the success of your food truck business. In this chapter, we'll explore the importance of supplier relationships, how to establish and maintain them, and the benefits they can bring to your business.

Establishing strong relationships with your suppliers can have a positive impact on every aspect of your food truck business. From ensuring the quality and consistency of your ingredients to negotiating better prices and terms, strong supplier relationships can help you run your business more efficiently and effectively.

Finding the right suppliers is the first step in building strong relationships. Look for suppliers that offer high-quality products, competitive prices, and reliable service. Consider attending trade shows and networking events to meet potential suppliers and learn more about their products and services.

Once you've found a supplier, it's important to communicate your needs and expectations. Be upfront about your budget, delivery requirements, and any special requests you may have. Establishing clear lines of communication from the outset can help prevent misunderstandings and ensure that both parties are on the same page.

Negotiating prices and terms with your suppliers is an important part of building a successful food truck business. Be prepared to negotiate on price, payment terms, and delivery schedules to get the best deal possible. However, it's also important to be fair and respectful in your negotiations, as a good relationship with your suppliers is built on mutual trust and respect.

Once you've established a relationship with a supplier, it's important to maintain it over time. This means staying in regular contact, providing feedback on their products and services, and being flexible and accommodating when necessary. Building a positive and mutually beneficial relationship with your suppliers can lead to long-term success for your food truck business.

Building strong relationships with your suppliers can bring several benefits to your food truck business. These include improved quality and consistency of ingredients, better pricing and terms, access to new products and innovations, increased reliability and responsiveness from suppliers, and enhanced reputation and credibility for your business.

Managing Inventory

Building strong relationships with your suppliers is a key component of running a successful food truck business. In this chapter, we'll explore why supplier relationships are important, how to build and maintain them, and the benefits they can bring to your business.

The Importance of Supplier Relationships

Supplier relationships are critical for food truck businesses for several reasons. First, they ensure a reliable supply of high-quality ingredients, which is essential for creating delicious and consistent menu items. Second, strong relationships can lead to better pricing and terms, helping you manage costs and improve your bottom line. Finally, good supplier relationships can lead to collaborations and innovations that can differentiate your food truck from competitors.

Finding the Right Suppliers

Finding the right suppliers is the first step in building strong relationships. Look for suppliers that offer high-quality products, competitive pricing, and reliable service. Consider factors such as proximity to your location, delivery schedules, and product availability when choosing suppliers. Attend trade shows, networking events, and industry conferences to meet potential suppliers and learn more about their offerings.

Communicating Effectively

Clear and open communication is key to building strong supplier relationships. Be transparent about your needs, expectations, and budget constraints. Provide feedback to your suppliers regularly, both positive and constructive, to help them understand your preferences and improve their service. Establishing a regular communication schedule can help you stay connected and address any issues that may arise promptly.

Building Trust and Reliability

Trust is the foundation of any successful relationship, including those with your suppliers. Be reliable in your orders and payments, and fulfill your commitments to your suppliers. Building a reputation as a trustworthy and dependable customer can lead to preferential treatment and better service from your suppliers.

Negotiating and Collaborating

Negotiating with your suppliers can help you secure better pricing and terms. However, it's important to approach negotiations as a collaboration rather than a confrontation. Look for mutually beneficial solutions that address the needs of both parties. Collaborating with your suppliers can also lead to innovations and improvements in your menu offerings.

Managing and Evaluating Suppliers

Managing your relationships with suppliers is an ongoing process. Regularly evaluate your suppliers based on criteria such as quality, pricing, and service. Consider conducting regular supplier audits to ensure that your suppliers are meeting your expectations and standards.

MARKETING AND BRANDING YOUR FOOD TRUCK

Creating a Unique Brand Identity

Creating a unique brand identity is essential for standing out in the competitive food truck industry. Your brand identity goes beyond your logo and color scheme; it's the personality and values that your business embodies. A strong brand identity can help build trust with customers, create a loyal following, and increase brand recognition.

To develop a strong brand identity, start by defining what makes your food truck unique. Consider your menu, your cooking style, and the experience you want to create for your customers. Your brand identity should be authentic and reflect the essence of your business.

Once you've defined your brand identity, design your brand elements, such as your logo, color scheme, and typography. These elements should be consistent across all of your marketing materials and convey the personality of your brand.

Your brand is more than just visual elements; it's also the experience you create for your customers. From the moment they see your food truck to the taste of your food, every interaction should reflect your brand's values and personality.

Promoting your brand is essential for attracting new customers and retaining existing ones. Use social media, events, and partnerships to promote your brand and engage with your target audience. Consider offering promotions or discounts to encourage customers to try your food and experience your brand.

To measure the success of your brand, track metrics such as customer satisfaction, brand awareness, and customer loyalty. Use this data to refine your brand strategy and ensure that your brand continues to resonate with your target audience.

Social Media and Online Presence

In today's digital age, having a strong social media presence is essential for the success of your food truck business. Social media allows you to connect with your customers, build brand awareness, and promote your products and services.

Creating a strong social media presence starts with choosing the right platforms for your business. Consider where your target audience spends their time online and focus your efforts on those platforms. Popular social media platforms for food truck businesses include Facebook, Instagram, Twitter, and TikTok.

Once you've chosen your platforms, create engaging and visually appealing content that showcases your food truck and menu items. Use high-quality images and videos to highlight your food and create mouth-watering content that will attract customers.

Engaging with your audience is key to building a loyal following on social media. Respond to comments and messages promptly, and interact with your followers by asking questions, running polls, and sharing user-generated content. This can help create a sense of community around your brand and encourage repeat business.

Social media is a powerful tool for promoting your food truck business. Use your platforms to announce your location and hours, promote daily specials and events, and offer promotions and discounts to attract customers. You can also use social media advertising to reach a larger audience and target specific demographics.

Your online reputation is crucial for attracting new customers and retaining existing ones. Monitor your social media channels regularly for feedback and reviews, and respond to both positive and negative comments professionally and promptly. This shows that you care about your customers' experiences and are committed to providing excellent service.

To measure the success of your social media efforts, track key metrics such as engagement, reach, and conversions. Use this data to refine your social media strategy and make informed decisions about your marketing efforts.

Promotions and Marketing Strategies

Promotions and marketing strategies are essential for attracting customers and growing your food truck business. In this chapter, we'll explore effective ways to promote your food truck, attract new customers, and build brand loyalty.

Understanding Your Target Audience

Before you can effectively promote your food truck, it's essential to understand your target audience. Consider factors such as demographics, preferences, and buying behaviors. This information will help you tailor your promotions and marketing strategies to appeal to your target audience.

Creating a Strong Brand Identity

A strong brand identity is crucial for standing out in the competitive food truck industry. Your brand identity encompasses everything from your logo and color scheme to your menu and customer service. Consistency is key, so ensure that your brand identity is reflected in all aspects of your business.

Utilizing Social Media

Social media is a powerful tool for promoting your food truck and engaging with your audience. Create engaging content that showcases your food and personality, and use social media platforms such as Facebook, Instagram, and Twitter to share updates, promotions, and behind-the-scenes glimpses of your business.

Partnering with Local Businesses and Events

Partnering with local businesses and events can help you reach new customers and expand your reach. Consider offering catering services for corporate events or teaming up with local breweries or wineries for special promotions. Participating in local festivals and events is another great way to promote your food truck and attract new customers.

Offering Promotions and Discounts

Promotions and discounts can help attract customers and encourage repeat business. Consider offering specials such as buy one, get one free deal, discounts for first-time customers, or loyalty programs for repeat customers. Promote these offers on social media and through other marketing channels to maximize their effectiveness.

Collecting Customer Feedback

Customer feedback is invaluable for improving your food truck business and marketing strategies. Encourage customers to provide feedback through surveys, comment cards, or social media polls. Use this feedback to make improvements and tailor your promotions to better meet the needs of your customers.

Analyzing and Adjusting Your Strategies

Finally, it's important to regularly analyze the effectiveness of your promotions and marketing strategies and adjust them as needed. Track key metrics such as sales, customer engagement, and return on investment to determine which strategies are working and which are not. Use this information to refine your approach and continue to grow your food truck business.

MANAGING OPERATIONS

Managing operations is a critical aspect of running a successful food truck business. In this chapter, we'll explore key strategies for managing your food truck operations efficiently and effectively, from planning your routes to ensuring food safety and managing finances.

Planning Your Routes

One of the first steps in managing your food truck operations is planning your routes. This involves identifying high-traffic areas where you can attract customers and mapping out your daily or weekly schedule. Consider factors such as location, time of day, and events happening in the area to maximize your sales potential.

Managing Inventory

Effective inventory management is essential for ensuring that you have enough supplies to meet demand without overstocking. Keep track of your inventory levels, monitor sales trends, and adjust your orders accordingly. This will help you minimize waste and maximize profitability.

Ensuring Food Safety

Food safety is paramount in the food truck industry. Follow best practices for food handling, storage, and preparation to prevent foodborne illnesses. Regularly inspect your food truck and equipment to ensure they meet health and safety standards.

Managing Finances

Managing your finances is crucial for the success of your food truck business. Keep track of your income and expenses, set a budget, and monitor your cash flow regularly. This will help you make informed decisions about pricing, promotions, and other aspects of your business.

Hiring and Managing Staff

If you have employees, hiring and managing them effectively is key to running a smooth operation. Clearly define roles and responsibilities, provide training and support, and communicate openly with your staff to ensure everyone is on the same page.

Marketing and Promotion

Marketing and promotion are essential for attracting customers to your food truck. Use social media, local advertising, and promotions to raise awareness of your business and attract new customers. Engage with your customers and collect feedback to improve your offerings and customer experience.

Adapting to Challenges

Running a food truck business comes with challenges, such as weather conditions, competition, and equipment failures. Stay flexible and be prepared to adapt to changing circumstances. Have a backup plan in place and be ready to make adjustments to your operations as needed.

Staffing Your Food Truck

Staffing your food truck is a crucial aspect of running a successful business. Your staff are the face of your business and play a significant role in delivering a positive customer experience. In this chapter, we'll explore key considerations for staffing your food truck, from hiring the right employees to managing and motivating your team.

Hiring the Right Employees

When hiring employees for your food truck, look for individuals who are passionate about food and customer service. Consider their experience, skills, and personality fit with your team. Conduct thorough interviews and background checks to ensure you hire the best candidates for the job.

Training and Development

Once you've hired your team, invest in their training and development. Provide comprehensive training on food preparation, safety protocols, customer service, and operating procedures. Ongoing training and development opportunities can help keep your team motivated and engaged.

Scheduling and Time Management

Efficient scheduling and time management are essential for ensuring that your food truck operates smoothly. Create a schedule that meets the needs of your business while also accommodating your employees' availability. Use tools and software to streamline scheduling and avoid conflicts.

Managing and Motivating Your Team

Effective team management involves setting clear expectations, providing regular feedback, and recognizing and rewarding your employees' contributions. Foster a positive work environment where your team feels valued and motivated to perform their best.

Dealing with Challenges

Running a food truck comes with its challenges, and your team will play a crucial role in helping you overcome them. Encourage open communication and problem-solving among your team members. Be supportive and proactive in addressing issues as they arise.

Ensuring Compliance with Labor Laws

As an employer, it's important to ensure compliance with labor laws and regulations. Familiarize yourself with relevant laws regarding wages, working hours, breaks, and safety standards. Stay updated on any changes to labor laws that may affect your business.

Promoting a Positive Work Culture

A positive work culture can help attract and retain top talent. Foster a culture of respect, collaboration, and innovation within your team. Encourage feedback and ideas from your employees, and celebrate successes together.

Customer Service and Engagement

Customer service and engagement are key aspects of running a successful food truck business. In this chapter, we'll explore strategies for providing exceptional customer service, engaging with your customers, and building lasting relationships that will keep them coming back for more.

Providing a positive customer experience starts with the first interaction a customer has with your food truck. Greet customers warmly, take the time to listen to their needs and ensure that their orders are prepared accurately and promptly. A friendly attitude and a smile can go a long way in creating a positive impression.

Building relationships with your customers is essential for building a loyal customer base. Get to know your regular customers by name, remember their preferences, and engage with them on a personal level. This can help create a sense of loyalty and keep them coming back to your food truck.

Feedback from your customers is invaluable for improving your products and services. Encourage customers to provide feedback through surveys, comment cards, or social media. Use this feedback to make improvements and tailor your offerings to better meet the needs of your customers.

No matter how well you run your food truck, you're bound to encounter the occasional unhappy customer. When handling customer complaints, listen attentively to their concerns, apologize for any mistakes, and offer a solution to resolve the issue. Handling complaints effectively can turn a negative experience into a positive one and help retain customers.

Social media is a powerful tool for engaging with your customers and building brand loyalty. Use social media platforms such as Facebook, Instagram, and Twitter to share updates, promotions, and behind-the-scenes glimpses of your food truck. Respond to comments and messages promptly, and engage with your followers to create a sense of community around your brand.

Rewarding your loyal customers can help keep them coming back for more. Consider offering loyalty programs, discounts for repeat customers, or special promotions for your social media followers. These incentives can help drive repeat business and encourage customers to spread the word about your food truck.

Managing Finances and Budgeting

Managing finances and budgeting are crucial skills for running a successful food truck business. In this chapter, we'll explore key strategies for managing your finances, creating a budget, and maximizing profitability.

Tracking Income and Expenses

One of the first steps in managing your finances is tracking your income and expenses. Keep detailed records of all your sales, expenses, and overhead costs. This will help you understand your cash flow and make informed decisions about your business.

Creating a Budget

Creating a budget is essential for managing your finances effectively. Estimate your monthly expenses, including food costs, fuel, equipment maintenance, and marketing expenses. Compare your budget to your actual expenses regularly to identify any discrepancies and make adjustments as needed.

Managing Cash Flow

Cash flow management is critical for the success of your food truck business. Keep track of your cash flow to ensure that you have enough money on hand to cover your expenses. Consider setting aside a portion of your revenue for unexpected expenses or slow periods.

Cost Control

Controlling costs is essential for maximizing profitability. Look for ways to reduce your expenses, such as buying ingredients in bulk, minimizing waste, and negotiating with suppliers for better prices. Monitor your costs regularly to identify areas where you can cut back.

Setting Prices

Setting prices for your menu items is a balancing act between covering your costs and remaining competitive. Consider factors such as food costs, overhead expenses, and the prices of similar items in your area. Regularly review your pricing strategy to ensure that it remains profitable.

Financial Planning

Financial planning is essential for the long-term success of your food truck business. Set financial goals for your business, such as increasing sales or expanding to new locations. Develop a plan for achieving these goals and track your progress regularly.

Seeking Professional Advice

Managing your finances can be challenging, especially if you're new to business ownership. Consider seeking advice from a financial advisor or accountant who can help you develop a financial strategy and manage your finances effectively.

GROWING YOUR FOOD TRUCK BUSINESS

Growing your food truck business requires careful planning and execution. In this chapter, we'll explore strategies for expanding your business, increasing your customer base, and maximizing your profits.

One way to grow your food truck business is by expanding your menu. Consider adding new and innovative items to attract new customers and keep your existing customers interested. Conduct market research to identify popular food trends and incorporate them into your menu.

Another strategy for growing your business is by exploring new locations. Consider attending events, festivals, and markets to reach a new audience. Research potential locations to ensure that they have enough foot traffic to make it worthwhile.

Collaborating with other businesses can help you reach a wider audience and grow your customer base. Consider partnering with local businesses to host events or offer special promotions. This can help increase your visibility and attract new customers.

Social media is a powerful tool for growing your food truck business. Use platforms like Facebook, Instagram, and Twitter to promote your business, engage with your customers, and share updates and promotions. Consider running targeted advertising campaigns to reach a larger audience.

Customer loyalty programs can help you retain your existing customers and encourage repeat business. Consider offering rewards for frequent purchases or discounts for loyal customers. This can help create a sense of loyalty and keep your customers coming back for more.

Expanding your catering services can be a lucrative way to grow your food truck business. Consider offering catering services for events, parties, and corporate functions. Develop a catering menu and marketing materials to promote your services to potential clients.

Investing in marketing and advertising can help you reach a larger audience and grow your business. Consider running targeted advertising campaigns, sponsoring local events, or partnering with influencers to promote your business. Track the effectiveness of your marketing efforts to ensure that you're getting a good return on your investment.

Growing your food truck business requires a combination of creativity, strategy, and hard work. By expanding your menu, exploring new locations, collaborating with other businesses, utilizing social media, implementing customer loyalty programs, expanding your catering services, and investing in marketing and advertising, you can attract new customers, retain existing ones, and maximize your profits. With careful planning and execution, your food truck business can continue to grow and thrive in a competitive market.

Adding Additional Locations or Trucks

Expanding your food truck business by adding additional locations or trucks can be a lucrative way to grow your customer base and increase your profits. In this chapter, we'll explore the benefits of expanding, how to choose the right locations, and how to manage multiple trucks effectively.

Benefits of Adding Additional Locations or Trucks

Adding additional locations or trucks can help you reach a wider audience and increase your visibility. It can also help you serve more customers and increase your revenue. By expanding, you can capitalize on new markets and opportunities for growth.

Choosing the Right Locations

When choosing additional locations for your food truck, it's important to consider factors such as foot traffic, demographics, and competition. Conduct market research to identify potential locations that are underserved and have a high demand for your offerings. Consider partnering with local businesses or events to increase your visibility and attract more customers.

Managing Multiple Trucks

Managing multiple trucks can be challenging, but with the right strategies, it can be a rewarding endeavor. Consider implementing systems and processes to streamline operations and ensure consistency across all trucks. Develop a schedule for each truck to ensure that they are serving different locations at the right times.

Marketing Your Additional Locations or Trucks

Marketing plays a crucial role in promoting your additional locations or trucks. Use social media to announce the opening of your new locations or trucks and engage with your customers. Consider offering promotions or discounts to incentivize customers to visit your new locations or trucks. Collaborate with local influencers or food bloggers to generate buzz and attract more customers.

Managing Costs

Expanding your business can also increase your costs, so it's important to manage them effectively. Keep track of your expenses and adjust your budget accordingly. Consider implementing cost-saving measures, such as buying ingredients in bulk or sharing resources between trucks, to reduce your overhead.

Building a loyal customer base

Building a loyal customer base is essential for the success of your food truck business. In this chapter, we'll explore strategies for attracting and retaining customers, creating a positive customer experience, and building relationships with your customers.

Creating a Positive Customer Experience

Providing exceptional customer service is key to building a loyal customer base. Greet your customers with a smile, take the time to listen to their needs, and ensure that their orders are accurate and delivered promptly. Engage with your customers and make them feel valued and appreciated.

Offering High-Quality Products

The quality of your food is crucial to building a loyal customer base. Use fresh, high-quality ingredients and prepare your food with care and attention to detail. Consider offering unique and innovative menu items to differentiate yourself from your competitors and attract new customers.

Building Relationships with Customers

Building relationships with your customers can help you create a loyal following. Take the time to get to know your customers and their preferences. Consider offering personalized recommendations or special promotions to reward their loyalty. Engage with your customers on social media and respond to their feedback and reviews to show that you value their input.

Rewarding Loyalty

Rewarding your loyal customers can help you retain them and encourage repeat business. Consider implementing a loyalty program where customers can earn points or rewards for their purchases. Offer special discounts or promotions to loyal customers to show your appreciation for their continued support.

Collecting Feedback

Collecting feedback from your customers can help you improve your products and services and build a stronger relationship with them. Encourage your customers to provide feedback through surveys or comment cards. Use their feedback to make improvements to your menu, service, and overall customer experience.

Engaging with the Community

Engaging with the community can help you build a positive reputation and attract new customers. Consider participating in local events, festivals, and markets to promote your business and reach a wider audience. Partner with local businesses or organizations to host events or fundraisers to support the community.

ADAPTING TO CHALLENGES AND TRENDS

Adapting to challenges and trends is crucial for the success of your food truck business. In this chapter, we'll explore how to identify and overcome challenges, as well as how to stay ahead of trends to keep your business thriving.

Identifying Challenges

Running a food truck business comes with its own set of challenges. Common challenges include finding the right location, managing inventory and costs, dealing with competition, and complying with regulations. It's important to identify these challenges early on and develop strategies to address them.

Overcoming Challenges

To overcome challenges, you need to be proactive and adaptable. For example, if finding a good location is a challenge, consider partnering with local businesses or events to increase your visibility. If managing inventory and costs is a challenge, implement inventory management systems and cost-saving measures.

Embracing Technology

Technology can help you streamline your operations and improve your customer experience. Consider using mobile ordering apps or accepting mobile payments to make it easier for customers to purchase from your food truck. Use social media to promote your business and engage with your customers.

Building a Strong Brand

Building a strong brand can help you stand out in a competitive market. Develop a unique and memorable brand identity that reflects your values and resonates with your target audience. Use social media and other marketing channels to communicate your brand story and connect with your customers.

Dealing with Seasonality and Weather

Dealing with seasonality and weather is a significant consideration for any food truck business. In this chapter, we'll discuss strategies for managing these challenges and ensuring your business remains successful throughout the year.

Understanding Seasonality

Seasonality refers to the fluctuations in customer demand and sales that occur throughout the year. In the food truck industry, seasonality can be influenced by factors such as weather, holidays, and local events. It's important to understand the seasonal trends in your area and adjust your business strategy accordingly.

Expanding Your Offerings

Another strategy for dealing with seasonality is to expand your offerings beyond traditional food truck fare. Consider offering seasonal specials, such as holiday-themed dishes or drinks, to attract customers during slower periods. You could also consider partnering with local businesses or events to offer catering services or participate in festivals or markets.

Managing Your Finances

Seasonality can also impact your finances, as your revenue may fluctuate throughout the year. It's important to budget carefully and set aside funds during peak seasons to help cover expenses during slower periods. Consider offering promotions or discounts during off-peak times to attract customers and boost sales.

Weathering the Storm: Dealing with Inclement Weather

Weather can also impact your business, especially if you operate in an area prone to extreme weather conditions. It's important to have a plan in place for dealing with inclement weather, such as rain or snow. Consider investing in equipment, such as awnings or heaters, to keep your customers comfortable during adverse weather conditions.

Staying Ahead of Food Trends

Staying ahead of food trends is essential for any food truck business looking to attract and retain customers. In this chapter, we'll explore strategies for identifying and capitalizing on the latest food trends to keep your business relevant and thriving.

Understanding Food Trends

Food trends are constantly evolving, driven by factors such as changing consumer preferences, health and wellness trends, and cultural influences. To stay ahead of food trends, it's important to stay informed about the latest developments in the food industry and be willing to adapt your menu to meet the changing demands of your customers.

Researching Food Trends

One of the best ways to stay ahead of food trends is to research and monitor industry publications, blogs, and social media channels for information about the latest food trends. Pay attention to what other food trucks, restaurants, and chefs are doing, and be open to experimenting with new ingredients and flavors.

Experimenting with New Flavors and Ingredients

Don't be afraid to experiment with new flavors and ingredients to create unique and innovative dishes that set your food truck apart from the competition. Consider incorporating seasonal and locally sourced ingredients into your menu to appeal to customers looking for fresh and sustainable options.

Offering Health-Conscious Options

Health and wellness trends are driving many food choices today, so consider offering health-conscious options on your menu. This could include gluten-free, vegetarian, or vegan options, as well as dishes that are low in fat, sugar, or calories. Be transparent about the ingredients you use and consider offering nutritional information for your dishes.

Creating Instagram-Worthy Dishes

In the age of social media, the presentation of your dishes is just as important as the taste. Create Instagram-worthy dishes that are visually appealing and photogenic to attract customers who are looking for unique and shareable dining experiences. Consider using creative plating techniques and vibrant colors to make your dishes stand out.

Collaborating with Other Businesses

Collaborating with other businesses can be a great way to stay ahead of food trends and reach new customers. Consider partnering with local breweries, wineries, or food producers to create unique and exclusive offerings that appeal to a broader audience.

Overcoming Common Challenges in the Food Truck Industry

Running a successful food truck business comes with its own set of challenges. From finding the right location to managing inventory and attracting customers, there are many obstacles that food truck owners must overcome. In this chapter, we'll explore some of the most common challenges faced by food truck owners and discuss strategies for overcoming them.

Finding the Right Location

One of the biggest challenges for food truck owners is finding the right location to park their trucks. The location can greatly impact the success of your business, as it determines the amount of foot traffic and visibility your truck will receive. To overcome this challenge, consider researching different locations and experimenting with different spots to see which ones are the most profitable.

Managing Inventory

Another common challenge for food truck owners is managing inventory. It can be difficult to predict how much food to prepare each day, leading to either waste or running out of popular items. To overcome this challenge, consider implementing inventory management software to track your inventory levels and sales data. This can help you make more informed decisions about how much food to prepare each day.

Attracting Customers

Attracting customers can be a challenge for food truck owners, especially in competitive markets. To overcome this challenge, consider using social media to promote your truck and engage with your customers. You could also consider offering promotions or discounts to attract new customers and keep them coming back.

Dealing with Seasonality

Seasonality can also be a challenge for food truck owners, as sales can fluctuate depending on the time of year. To overcome this challenge, consider offering seasonal specials or catering services to generate additional revenue during slower periods. You could also consider partnering with local events or businesses to increase your visibility during peak seasons.

Complying with Regulations

Complying with regulations can be a challenge for food truck owners, as there are often strict rules and regulations governing where and how food trucks can operate. To overcome this challenge, familiarize yourself with the regulations in your area and ensure that your truck meets all health and safety requirements. Consider joining a food truck association or network to stay informed about any changes to regulations.

Running a food truck business can be challenging, but by understanding and overcoming these common challenges, you can increase your chances of success. By finding the right location, managing inventory effectively, attracting customers, dealing with seasonality, and complying with regulations, you can build a thriving food truck business that stands out in a competitive market.

CONCLUSION

Starting a food truck business from scratch requires careful planning, dedication, and a willingness to adapt to the challenges of the industry. From finding the right concept and menu to navigating the legal and regulatory landscape, each step of the process presents its own set of challenges and opportunities for growth.

For beginners, the key is to start small and focus on building a loyal customer base. This means finding the right location, offering high-quality food at competitive prices, and using social media and other marketing strategies to attract customers. It also means being prepared to face challenges such as managing inventory, dealing with seasonality, and complying with regulations.

As you gain experience and grow your business, you can start to expand your menu, add additional locations or trucks, and explore new ways to attract customers. This might include offering catering services, partnering with local events or businesses, or experimenting with new food trends and flavors.

Throughout the process, it's important to stay flexible and open to new ideas. The food truck industry is constantly evolving, and what works today may not work tomorrow. By staying informed about industry trends and consumer preferences, you can position your business for long-term success.

Finally, building a successful food truck business requires passion and perseverance. There will inevitably be setbacks and challenges along the way, but by staying focused on your goals and continuously striving to improve, you can overcome these obstacles and build a thriving business that brings joy and satisfaction to both you and your customers.

Starting a food truck business can be a rewarding venture, but it comes with its own set of challenges. From finding the right location to managing inventory and attracting customers, there are many factors to consider. In this recap, we'll summarize the key points discussed in this guide on how to start a food truck business, from beginner to pro.

Finding the Right Location: One of the first steps in starting a food truck business is finding the right location. Consider factors such as foot traffic, visibility, and parking regulations when choosing a location for your truck. It's also important to research the local market to understand the demand for your food offerings in different areas.

Obtaining Permits and Licenses: Before you can start operating your food truck, you'll need to obtain the necessary permits and licenses. This includes health permits, business licenses, and any other permits required by your local government. Make sure to research the requirements in your area and budget for any associated costs.

Developing a Business Plan: A well-thought-out business plan is essential for success in the food truck industry. Your business plan should outline your target market, menu offerings, pricing strategy, and marketing plan. It should also include financial projections to help you track your progress and make informed decisions.

Choosing the Right Truck or Trailer: The type of truck or trailer you choose can have a big impact on your food truck business. Consider factors such as size, layout, and equipment when choosing a truck. It's also important to budget for any modifications or upgrades needed to customize your truck to suit your needs.

Equipment and Supplies: Equipping your food truck with the right equipment and supplies is essential for success. This includes cooking equipment, refrigeration, serving utensils, and cleaning supplies. Make sure to invest in high-quality equipment that can withstand the rigors of the road.

Menu Development: Developing a menu that showcases your culinary skills and appeals to your target market is crucial. Consider factors such as food costs, preparation time, and popularity when designing your menu. It's also important to regularly update your menu to keep things fresh and exciting for your customers.

Marketing and Promotion: Marketing and promotion are key to attracting customers to your food truck. Use social media, food truck events, and local advertising to promote your business. Offering promotions and discounts can also help attract new customers and keep them coming back.

Managing Operations: Managing the day-to-day operations of your food truck is essential for success. This includes everything from food preparation and service to inventory management and customer service. Develop systems and processes to streamline your operations and ensure consistency.

Financial Management: Managing your finances is critical for the success of your food truck business. Keep track of your expenses, revenue, and profits to ensure you're on track to meet your financial goals. Consider working with an accountant or financial advisor to help you manage your finances effectively.

Starting a food truck business can be challenging, but with careful planning and execution, you can build a successful and profitable business. By following the steps outlined in this guide, you can navigate the challenges of the food truck industry and turn your passion for food into a thriving business.

www.ingramcontent.com/pod-product-compliance
Lightning Source LLC
Chambersburg PA
CBHW070412230526
45471CB00006B/2764